CLOCKS AND HOW THEY GO

by Gail Gibbons

Thomas Y. Crowell   New York

To Guy, the musical timekeeper

For information address Thomas Y. Crowell, 10 East 53 Street,
New York, N. Y. 10022. Published simultaneously in Canada by
Fitzhenry & Whiteside Limited, Toronto.

Library of Congress Cataloging in Publication Data

Gibbons, Gail.
Clocks and how they go.
SUMMARY: Describes the weight clock and the
spring clock and how they work.
1.Clocks and watches—Juvenile literature.
[1. Clocks and watches] I. Title.
TS542.5.G52 1979   681'.113   78-22498
ISBN 0-690-03973-5   ISBN 0-690-03974-3 lib. bdg.
First Edition

There are many different kinds of clocks, but they all do the same thing. They show us what time it is.

People didn't always have clocks. At first, they told time from nature. They studied the motion of the stars at night and checked the moving shadow on their sundials during the day.

They watched candles, water clocks, and sandglasses.
But these couldn't keep correct time, and they were
a lot of trouble. Candles had to be replaced as
soon as they burned down, water clocks had to be
filled up again when the water ran out, and
sandglasses had to be turned over so the sand
could run through again. The old ways of telling
time were not good enough.

Nearly 700 years ago, the first mechanical clock,
a clock with moving parts, was made. It kept better
time and wasn't so much trouble to keep going.
This clock had no hands at all. It told the time by
chiming bells. Other early clocks had just one hand,
an hour hand.

We use mechanical clocks today. There are two kinds of mechanical clocks, the weight clock and the spring clock. The weight clock was the first kind to be made.

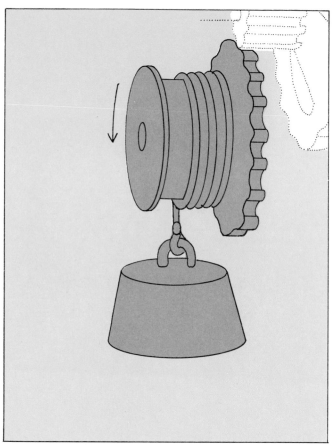

The weight clock has a weight inside that hangs
from a cord. The other end of the cord is wound
around a small drum. When the cord is fully wound,
the weight is up high. As the weight drops, it turns
the drum. The turning drum moves the parts
of the clock to make the clock go.

Fastened to the back end of the drum is a wheel
called the main wheel. When the drum turns, the
main wheel turns with it. The tiny teeth on its
outside fit the teeth at the inside of the next
wheel, the center wheel. When the main wheel
turns, it makes the center wheel turn.

The center wheel makes the next wheel turn.
The teeth on its outside fit the next wheel's inside
teeth. This is called meshing.

That wheel makes still other wheels turn when they
mesh their teeth. All the wheels turning together
turn the hands of the clock to tell the time. Some
clocks have one or two more wheels than other clocks,
but all clocks have a main wheel, a center wheel,
and at least one other wheel.

But a weight clock needs something else to help it keep correct time. It needs a pendulum.
The pendulum slows down the moving parts.
It keeps the weight from falling too fast and the hands from turning too fast.

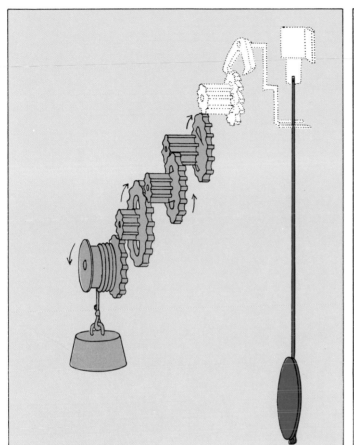

The pendulum is a long rod with a round plate, called a bob, at the bottom end. The top of the rod is attached to a bar with a hook at each end. The bar is called a pallet fork and the hooks are called pallets.

Below the pallet fork is a wheel called an escape
wheel, with specially shaped teeth. The pallet
fork, the escape wheel, and the pendulum together
are called the escapement.

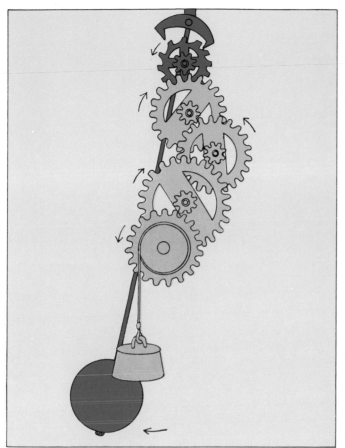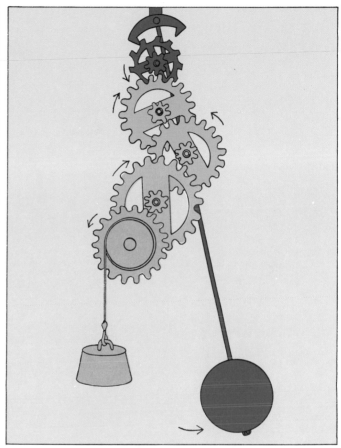

The escape wheel turns with all the other wheels
of the clock. As it turns, its teeth are stopped
by the pallets on the pallet fork, first one pallet
and then the other. The pallet fork tips one way
and then the other way, and the pendulum swings
back and forth.

As the pendulum goes back and forth, back and forth, the escape wheel moves forward only one tooth at a time. The escape wheel slows down all the wheels that turn the hands of the clock and the clock tells the right time.

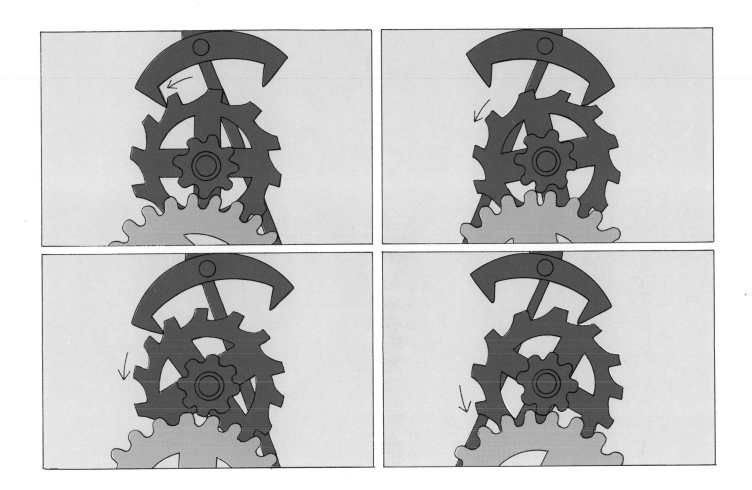

As the pallets move in and out of the escape wheel, the clock goes tick-tock, tick-tock. Each tick-tock is one second in time.

The weight clock is a large clock because of the
space needed for the weight and the pendulum.
The spring clock was made because people wanted
smaller clocks and watches.

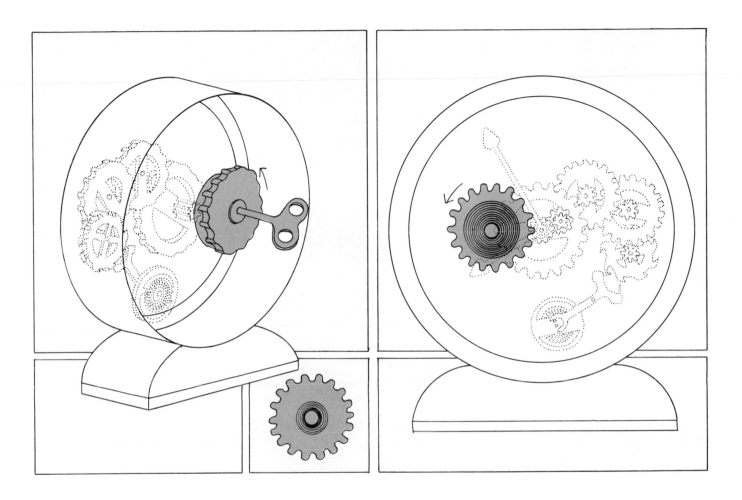

Instead of a weight, a spring clock has a spring inside, called a mainspring. When the mainspring is wound, it gets very tight. As the mainspring unwinds, it moves the parts of the clock.

The mainspring is attached to the main wheel. As it unwinds, the main wheel turns with it. The main wheel makes the center wheel turn and the center wheel turns the next wheel. Each wheel turns a next wheel when they mesh. The wheels turn the hands of the clock to tell the time.

But a spring clock needs something else to help it tell the right time. Instead of a pendulum, many spring clocks have a balance wheel. The balance wheel slows down the other wheels. It keeps the mainspring from unwinding too fast and the hands from turning too fast.

There is a tiny spring fixed to the balance wheel.
When the wheel turns, the spring is tightened.
As the spring unwinds, it pushes the wheel back
again. So the balance wheel turns one way and then
the other way, just as a pendulum in a weight clock
swings back and forth.

The balance wheel has a lever loosely fixed to its center. As the wheel turns, it moves the lever back and forth. As the lever goes back and forth, tiny pallets on its other end move in and out of the teeth of an escape wheel. The lever, the escape wheel, and the balance wheel are the spring clock's escapement.

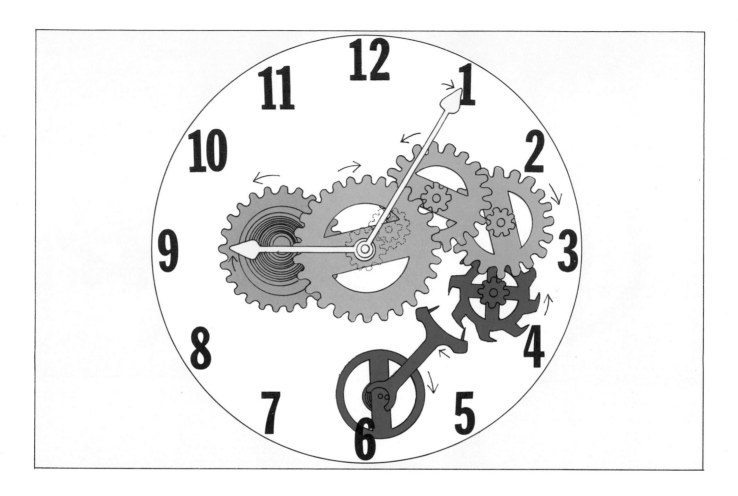

The pallets on the lever let go only one tooth at a time, so the escape wheel moves slowly. All the wheels of the clock slow down, the hands slow down, and the clock shows the right time.

As the pallets move in and out of the teeth of the escape wheel, the clock goes tick-tick-tick-tick-tick. There are usually five ticks to each second in time.

Some spring clocks use a pendulum instead of a balance wheel to keep the hands turning at just the right speed. These are bigger spring clocks.

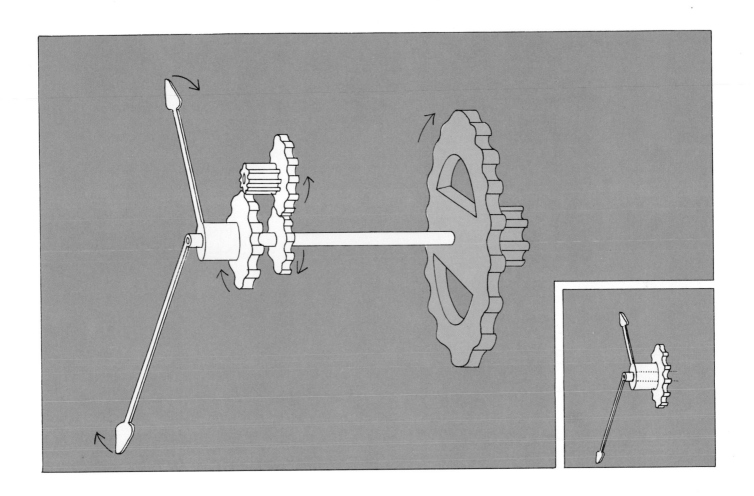

But how come the minute hand of a clock goes around twelve times while the hour hand goes around only once? The minute hand is connected directly to the main wheel. It turns as fast as the main wheel turns. The hour hand is connected to an extra set of wheels that slow it down.

Nowadays we have electric clocks. Instead of a weight or spring to make the parts move, an electric clock has a motor that runs by electricity. The motor moves the wheels and the wheels turn the hands to tell the right time.

A battery clock runs on the energy in a battery.
Electric or battery clocks don't go tick-tock or
tick-tick-tick-tick-tick because they don't have
escapements to control the speed of the hands.
They make a humming sound. A digital clock uses
electricity or a battery, but instead of hands it has
changing numbers to show the time. Digital clocks
are mostly very quiet.

That's how clocks go... and clocks can tick-tock, or tick-tick-tick-tick-tick, or hum, or make no noise at all.

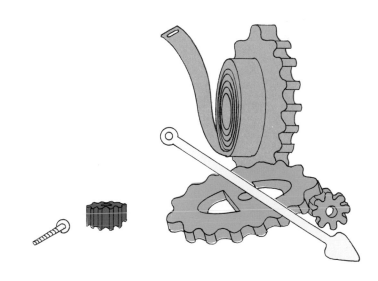

The Parts of a Clock

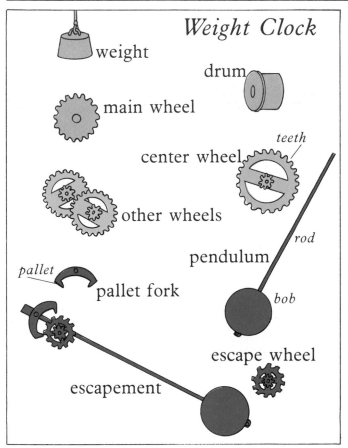

Weight Clock

weight

drum

main wheel

center wheel

teeth

other wheels

rod

pendulum

pallet

pallet fork

bob

escape wheel

escapement

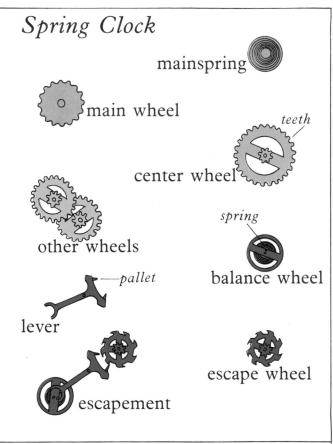

Spring Clock

mainspring

main wheel

teeth

center wheel

spring

other wheels

balance wheel

pallet

lever

escape wheel

escapement

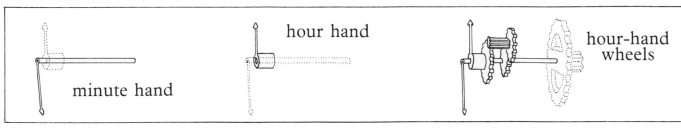

minute hand

hour hand

hour-hand wheels